YOU CHOOSE

# CAN YOU SURVIVE A ROARING TORNADO?

## An Interactive Survival Adventure

by Thomas Kingsley Troupe

CAPSTONE PRESS
a capstone imprint

Published by Capstone Press, an imprint of Capstone
1710 Roe Crest Drive, North Mankato, Minnesota 56003
capstonepub.com



Library of Congress Cataloging-in-Publication Data is available on the Library of Congress website.
ISBN: 9798875240683 (hardcover)
ISBN: 9798875240652 (paperback)
ISBN: 9798875240669 (ebook PDF)

Summary: You Choose lets YOU control the story! Readers choose their own paths while encountering tornadoes in three different scenarios. The outcomes are different as decisions are made throughout the book.

Editorial Credits
Editor: Carrie Sheely; Designer: Heidi Thompson; Media Researcher: Rebekah Hubstenberger; Production Specialist: Tori Abraham

Image Credits
Getty Images: Bettmann,102; Shutterstock: 4Max, 18, Animaflora PicsStock, 26, Artacke Pictures, 25, Darryl Brooks, 20, desdemona72, 103, Domenichini Giuliano, 62, EmiliaUngur, 67, Ionela5Mocanu, cover, Little Adventures, 33, Lukas Jonaitis, 45, Minerva Studio, 52, rangizzz, 90, ribbonpink, 47, Robert Harding Video, 76, Sabphoto, 86, Sahara Prince, 40, 71, SingerGM, 58, swa182, 83, Triff, 15, Vahagni, 98, Wiparat P (texture background), back cover and throughout



Printed and bound in China. 006461

# TABLE OF CONTENTS

INTRODUCTION

# ABOUT YOUR ADVENTURE

YOU are going about your daily life when a tornado strikes. With wind, flying debris, and unstable structures, danger comes from all directions. It's going to take quick thinking and smart choices to survive the storm and its aftermath. YOU CHOOSE what path to take. Will you stay grounded and alive or be overtaken by the swirling storm?

Chapter One sets the scene. Then you choose which path to read. Follow the directions at the bottom of the page. Your decisions will change your outcome. After you finish one path, go back and read the others for new perspectives and more adventures.

*Turn the page to begin your adventure.*

## CHAPTER 1

# A LITTLE RAIN

You woke up early this morning to what seemed like a normal day. The weather has been humid and sticky, more so than usual. You see large, tall clouds off in the distance. They're a little dark, and rain seems likely.

*A little rain never hurt anyone,* you think.

Less than an hour later, the clouds in the horizon have grown much darker. You wonder if the storm will head your way. You never minded a little rain, but a storm is a completely different story.

Checking the sky ten minutes later, you realize you're out of luck. The storm is building and getting close. The sky's color seems a bit off.

*Turn the page.*

"Great," you say to yourself. A storm is *not* what you need today. The storm appears to be severe. Booms of thunder rumble across the horizon. Lightning flashes behind the clouds. The rain sprinkles grow steadier. If it keeps up, you might have to take shelter.

Then the storm seems to stop. The sky almost looks green. In the distance, you hear a sound like a locomotive. You scan the sky. A small funnel shape is forming at the bottom of the low, dark clouds. A tornado is coming! So much for a little rain!

*To be a sheriff on patrol in the central United States, turn to page 11.*

*To be an Irish sheep farmer, turn to page 43.*

*To join your cousins on an Argentinean road trip, turn to page 75.*

# WHAT ARE TORNADOES?

Tornadoes are dangerous storms that occur when moist, warm air combines with dry, cold air. The mixture causes powerful winds to spin. The spinning storms can tear apart buildings, uproot trees, and cause other damage. Entire towns can be left in ruins. They also can injure or kill people.

Tornadoes can form anywhere. But they are most likely to form in the central part of the United States between March and June. About 1,000 tornadoes strike the United States each year. Tornadoes also occur in Australia, Canada, South America, and parts of Europe.

CHAPTER 2

# SERVE AND PROTECT

Before your brother moved away three years ago, he said nothing exciting ever happens in this sleepy Kansas town. As sheriff, very little happening is exactly what you hope for.

You step out of Martha's Home Cookin' Café on Saturday afternoon. Your patrol vehicle waits at the curb, the engine running. It's ready if something exciting *does* happen.

"Afternoon Sheriff," longtime resident Abe Greeley says. "How's your day going?"

*Turn the page.*

"So far so good," you reply.

"Feel that storm coming?" Abe asks.

Before you can shake your head, a drop of rain hits your hand. Skies were mostly blue when you went in for lunch. Now its darkening by the moment.

"I do now," you say with a smile.

"Sure don't like the look of those clouds," Abe whispers, following your gaze.

The clouds rumble. More rain falls, faster and harder than before.

"Better get in for your lunch," you suggest, nodding to Martha's. "Hopefully it'll clear up before you get the check."

Abe chuckles and ducks into Martha's Café. You quickly dash to your patrol vehicle and climb inside. A wet uniform is no fun.

Heavy rain pelts the windshield. Lightning flashes and thunder rolls. You turn on the wiper blades to clear your view. Small ice pellets tap at your car's window and hood.

*Hail.*

You're unsure how bad the storm will get. You could patrol the streets in case things get ugly. It would be good to advise people to seek shelter.

Then again, it could be a storm that doesn't become severe and passes through quickly. You could head back to the station and respond to calls from there.

You grab the walkie-talkie and decide.

*To let dispatch know you're resuming patrol, turn to page 14.*

*To let dispatch know you're heading back to the station, turn to page 16.*

“Sheriff to dispatch,” you say through the handset.

“Go ahead,” Rudy replies from the station.

“Just advising, storm’s picking up,” you respond. “So far, it’s just light hail.”

“Copy,” Rudy replies. “Saw that, Sheriff. Radar got really colorful on me. Might get rough out there.”

You patrol a few blocks as the storm continues to build. People on the sidewalk look to the sky from beneath storefront awnings. You look through your driver’s side window.

The clouds above have a strange, greenish tint to them. In the horizon, a small funnel shape is forming. Within moments, you can hear an ominous sound.

“Sounds like a train!” an older boy shouts.

*A tornado is coming,* you think. Time to act!

You remember there are baseball playoffs happening at the high school. It might be a good idea to head over there to make sure everyone takes shelter.

You look up to see a family of four ahead. They are waving you down from the sidewalk.

*To see what the family on the sidewalk needs, turn to page 19.*

*To head to the baseball field, turn to page 30.*

The hail comes down harder than ever as you head toward the station.

"Sheriff to dispatch," you begin.

"Go ahead," Rudy replies.

"Going to get out of the storm for a bit," you say.

"Oh," Rudy said. "10-4. See you back here soon, Sheriff."

You're back at the station in minutes. You pull into the garage and park in your reserved spot.

You climb out, check the car, and are happy to see the hail hasn't done any serious damage. The rain continues to pour as you enter the sheriff's office.

Once inside, Rudy looks up from his three computer monitors.

Ashley, one of the deputies, seems surprised to see you.

"Pretty bad out there," you say, breaking the silence.

But when you glance out the window again, the rain has stopped. Yet in the distance, the sky is a sickly shade of green.

"Well," you reply. "I hope that's not what I think it is."

You don't want to cause unnecessary concern, so you walk to the front for a better look. Water drips from the gutters, but the rain has ceased. You step out onto the front sidewalk.

You hear a locomotive sound in the distance. Elsewhere, that would be fine, but trains don't pass through this town.

The noise means one thing and it turns out it's *exactly* what you thought it was. A tornado is coming!

*Turn the page.*

You're about to dash inside the station and head to the basement. But just then, you see a teenage boy and girl running down the street. Maybe you should tell them to come in the sheriff's office with you first.

*To head for the basement to take shelter, turn to page 26.*

*To tell the passersby to come inside, turn to page 28.*

*Why haven't you heard the sirens?* you wonder. Whenever there's a major storm, the sirens sound. But today there's nothing!

You pull up to the family on the sidewalk. They quickly run toward you.

"Sheriff," the man cries. "We've locked our keys in our car! And this weather looks ugly. Can you help?"

"Never mind the car," you shout. "There's a tornado coming! Get in, and I'll get you out of this!"

The family climbs into your patrol car. Once they're inside, something heavy slams into the side of your car. Your passengers cry out in surprise. A metal newspaper box tumbles down the street.

Garbage from a tipped trash can peppers the car as you put the vehicle into drive. The tornado is close. Too close.

*Turn the page.*

Just then, the sirens sound. *Better late than never,* you think.

"Where are we going?" the woman in the passenger seat cries. Her kids are trying to touch her hand through the back seat partition.

You have a few choices. The elementary school is just ahead. Or you could drive a bit farther and bring them to the sheriff's office.

*To bring the family to the sheriff's office, go to page 21.*

*To head to the school for shelter, turn to page 22.*

"Let's get you back to the station," you decide. You call in to Rudy and let him know you're headed back.

"Roger that, Sheriff," Rudy replies. "Be careful."

You're grateful that the roads are mostly clear and everyone else seems to be off the streets. You pull into the parking garage, and Rudy comes out to bring the family in. You can hear the wind whistling along the outside of the building. *Clunk! Thunk!* Debris hits the exterior walls.

It's getting bad out there.

The family thanks you for helping them before heading inside. Rudy stops and looks back at you in the squad car. "You coming too, Sheriff?"

You could take shelter in the station. But what if someone else out there needs your help?

*To head back out into the storm and continue patrolling, turn to page 32.*

*To get out and seek shelter inside the station, turn to page 34.*

The brick school building seems best. You race down Main Street, swerving as a section of wooden fence flies in front of you. It tumbles once on the street then smashes a minivan's windows.

A teenage boy looks like he's recording the storm with his phone.

"Seek shelter," you order, using the car's PA system. You hope any people on the street can hear you over the wild winds.

You drive onto the front lawn of the elementary school. The playground's swings fly and rattle around the swing set. Wood chips lift and swirl into the sky.

You park, exit the car, and open the back door. From somewhere nearby, you hear big explosions. It sounds like power transformers being destroyed in the tornado's path.

"Quickly!" you shout, leading the family to the school's entrance.

The boy reaches the door and tugs the handle. The door doesn't budge.

"It won't open!" the boy shouts.

"There's no school on Saturday," the girl cries.

Behind you, the winds pick up. Tree branches and roofing shingles fly around.

You could break into the school if there's enough time. You glance at nearby Sunny Park and spot a picnic pavilion there. It won't make a great shelter. But it might be the only structure you can get to before the wind picks up even more.

*To break into the school and seek shelter, turn to page 24.*

*To run to the picnic pavilion, turn to page 36.*

There's no time to find somewhere else. You didn't expect to commit breaking and entering as a sheriff, but the situation demands it.

You pull your flashlight from your belt and use it to smash a pane of glass on the metal door. It shatters and you knock out the remaining shards.

"Hurry!" the little girl cries.

You see nearby utility poles snap like twigs. Sparks fly as power lines tear free from transformers.

You reach inside and push the door bar, opening it with a click.

"Get in," you shout, holding the door open. "And head downstairs to the hallways near the gym!"

The kids nod, familiar with the school. They lead their parents through the dark hallways. You're about to join them before spotting something run past Good Sun Grocery.

It's a small, black dog. It's Mr. Rawling's beloved Mitzy.

"Mitzy!" you shout, hoping the dog hears you. Your voice sounds weak in the roaring wind.

Mitzy stops near a downed garbage can. Her tail wags as she finds something tasty in the trash.

The tornado is getting closer. You could risk it and grab Mitzy to rescue her. You know how much the dog means to your friend. But there may not be enough time.

*To run across the street to save Mitzy, turn to page 38.*

*To follow the family into the school's basement, turn to page 40.*

There's no time to lose. You dash into the sheriff's office.

"Downstairs," you order. "Now!"

"You don't have to tell me twice," Rudy cries.

Something crashes as you reach the basement entrance. The glass front door has exploded. Deadly debris flies into the station as the wind scatters papers. Peterson's Hardware store across the street is demolished in an explosion of wood.

Wishing you could do more, you follow Ashley into the basement. You close the heavy door behind you.

The three of you huddle near the storage shelves away from the windows. The whole building vibrates and shakes. You glance up, expecting the ceiling to disappear at any moment.

Furniture is tossed around upstairs, making loud thumps above you. You wonder what your department will look like when the storm is over.

The lights flicker, and a moment later, they're out completely.

"Generator should kick in," Rudy whispers in the dark.

You click on your flashlight. The tornado is bad, but you'll survive.

You just hope the citizens you swore to protect will survive too.

## THE END

To follow another path, turn to page 8.
To learn more about tornadoes,
turn to page 101.

“Get indoors,” you shout. “Now!”

You usher them into the sheriff’s office.

You watch for others out in the storm. You find it hard to take your eyes away as the awesome spectacle of nature forms right in front of you. A large funnel shape appears beneath the low, gray clouds. Your eyes are fixed on it.

“Sheriff?” Rudy says from inside. “Maybe you ought to come in and head downstairs with us.”

You nod as debris flies around outside. Seconds later, tornado sirens sound, blaring across town.

“Well, that took a while,” Ashley says from inside. “There was hardly any time to react.”

“They can’t predict the weather,” you remind her. “They’re looking for long periods of high winds, funnel clouds, and a touchdown.”

You feel the high winds as you step inside. The steel door slams shut behind you, shattering the glass. Sticks and leaves blast through the opening, and your uniform pants flap like flags. You turn toward the staircase to get downstairs.

But you can't resist seeing the tornado. You watch the tornado closing in on the sheriff's office. In seconds, Peterson's Hardware store across the street is torn to shreds. Shingles and aluminum siding fly up into the funnel.

Suddenly a piece of lumber crashes through your front window. The heavy wood slams into your head. In a flash, your world goes dark and silent.

**THE END**

To follow another path, turn to page 8.
To learn more about tornadoes, turn to page 101.

As you get closer to the baseball field, you see rows of cars. There are a lot of people at the baseball field. You need to warn them as soon as possible.

Just then, the siren sounds.

*Took them long enough,* you think. Now the people will know the storm is no joke. Hopefully they'll take shelter.

In your rearview mirror, a large tree bends and tips over. Its roots yank a large chunk of dirt from the ground. The leafy branches completely block the road.

You reach the baseball diamond. You're relieved to see players hopping into their parents' cars. They're driving off.

"Get to shelter immediately," you order over the PA. "Get off the roads as soon as possible."

In moments, the field is cleared. You notice someone lying on the ground alongside a bench. It looks like a player. It's hard to tell with all of the debris and rain.

"Get up," you shout. "There's a tornado coming."

*Did they leave someone behind?* you wonder. *Seriously?*

The kid doesn't get up. You park the cruiser and run out into the wind. You can barely move but push on. As you get closer, you realize it isn't a player. It's a bag full of baseball bats.

The tornado is upon you and the bat bag flies at you, striking you in the head. You are knocked unconscious before being thrown far and high. You do not survive the fall.

## THE END

To follow another path, turn to page 8.
To learn more about tornadoes,
turn to page 101.

There's a chance that someone else might be stuck outside in this horrible storm. You're not sure you'd be able to sleep at night knowing you didn't do everything you could to help.

"I need to do another pass through town," you tell Rudy. "I want to make sure the streets are clear."

Rudy raises his eyebrows and shakes his head. "You could just wait until we get a call, otherwise—"

"By then it'll be too late," you say, interrupting him. You drive off before he can say another word. Time is wasting!

You drive a few blocks away and the town looks like it's being ripped apart. Garbage and tree branches are everywhere. Lawn ornaments slam into your car, and a birdhouse bounces off the hood. The tornado is closer than ever.

You avoid the obstacles in the road and watch helplessly as the tornado rips through Lee's Hardware store. Chunks of metal, wood, and tools smash into your patrol car.

A moment later, your vehicle is lifted off the ground. It comes down two seconds later, landing on its side. The windows explode in a shower of glass.

In minutes, the tornado moves away, leaving you stuck in your car. You're battered and bruised but alive.

**THE END**

To follow another path, turn to page 8.
To learn more about tornadoes, turn to page 101.

The sounds outside the station's garage are getting louder and more intense. Going back out onto the streets would endanger yourself needlessly. Unless an actual emergency call comes in, you know you should stay put.

*I can't help anyone if I'm dead,* you remind yourself. It's something you learned back in law enforcement training.

"Yeah," you tell Rudy, shutting off the engine. "I'm coming in too."

You follow Rudy into the building and see the family. They're heading into the basement with Ashley, one of the deputies.

As you reach the door to the basement, you hear a loud crash. You look and see that the front window of the sheriff's office has shattered. A large branch has smashed through the glass, letting the wind in.

You hurry downstairs as the upper floor is torn apart. You all find spots near a concrete wall and wait out the tornado.

Within ten minutes, it's over. You and the others have survived.

## THE END

To follow another path, turn to page 8.
To learn more about tornadoes, turn to page 101.

You're not sure you'll be able to break through the window. It looks like strong, tempered glass and might just waste time.

You point to the picnic pavilion across the street. There's a large roof over the tables to provide shade on sunnier days.

"Head for those picnic tables under the pavilion!" you shout. The tables have posts cemented into the ground to prevent theft. They might just save your lives.

The family looks confused. They raise their arms to shield themselves from the flying debris.

"Hurry!" you shout.

You all run across the street. Everyone's clothes ripple in the wind. Power lines snap like twigs, making electrical light flashes. A utility pole tips over, smashing the transformer against the ground with a loud boom.

"Go, go!" you shout, urging them forward.

You help everyone climb beneath the picnic tables and hang onto the metal bars. Before you can climb under too, something heavy slams into your back. You tumble over a picnic table and land hard.

Dazed, you stand up as the tornado rips through Sunny Park.

"Sheriff!" the woman shouts. "Get down!"

Her warning comes too late. The roof of the pavilion lifts up, and suddenly you're in the air. You rise up off the ground, watching the picnic tables become a blur beneath. The pavilion's destroyed roof hits you hard. You go unconscious and never wake up before falling to the ground, hundreds of feet below.

**THE END**

To follow another path, turn to page 8.
To learn more about tornadoes,
turn to page 101.

You make a split-second decision to take the risk. You holster your flashlight while running toward the grocery store. As you get close, you see fallen utility poles lying on the ground. Loose power lines stretch across the street.

*Let's avoid those,* you think as you cut through the school's front lawn. Papers swirl and whip against your face. It's like jumbo confetti at a deadly parade.

You finally reach the sidewalk. A few blocks down, someone is shouting. You glance down Main Street and see the tornado rip through the center of town. Its path of destruction is incredible.

"Mitzy!" you shout, shielding your face from the wind and debris.

You reach the dog and try to scoop her up. Just then, the tipped garbage can clatters, startling the dog. She runs away, frightened.

*I was just trying to help,* you think. You know chasing after the dog is too risky. You hope Mitzy will be okay as you turn to race back to the school. As you do, you eye Main Street again. There are overturned cars, chunks of rooftops, and broken store signs littering the streets. As you marvel at the fading funnel cloud, you trip and fall into a puddle.

You didn't see the water was electrified by the downed power lines. Your body shakes violently, and you die in a matter of seconds as the storm ends.

## THE END

To follow another path, turn to page 8.
To learn more about tornadoes,
turn to page 101.

You'd love to save Mitzy, but it's too risky. You head into the school, hoping the pooch survives the storm.

The wind slams the door shut with a bang. You run quickly through the empty hallways.

You hear the wind outside howl and churn. Windows vibrate in the classrooms and further down the hall, something shatters.

You find the stairs to the basement and scramble down, two at a time.

You hear loud noises on the floor above. You suspect the high winds have blown out more windows. Desks and chairs are likely tumbling around the rooms.

Once in the basement, you see the family sitting against the hallway's bricks. Their heads are tucked down covered by their arms.

You join them. The little girl puts her hand on your wrist.

"Thank you, Sheriff," she whispers.

Outside the world is chaos, but you and the family are safe.

## THE END

To follow another path, turn to page 8.
To learn more about tornadoes, turn to page 101.

CHAPTER 3

# A FARMER'S FRIGHT

Your parents often told you that a farmer's work is never done, usually after complaining about doing chores around the farm. You and your brother, Evan, guessed your grandparents believed that too.

Turns out, they were right.

Your parents passed away years ago. You and Evan tend the family farm near Glenmast, Northern Ireland. The hills and valleys are too rocky for crops, but your sheep produce the finest wool in the United Kingdom.

*Turn the page.*

This morning, like all mornings, is full of things to do. Evan agreed to wake up early to help mend the fence, but his bedroom door remains closed.

You and Molly, your Kerry Blue Terrier, head outside to get started. After feeding the sheep, you let them out to pasture.

You hop onto your ATV and start the engine. You hope it wakes your brother.

Molly darts in circles, ready to run. You head away from the small, old farmhouse on a dirt trail.

The sky is mostly blue with scattered clouds. They're dark, but not enough to keep you inside.

Five minutes later, you reach the damaged fence. One of the rotted posts has broken into two, leaving a gap big enough to let a curious sheep out.

You get to work. Molly chases a squirrel and barks at a tree. You pull the old wood from the ground as random raindrops fall.

You're unsure how much time has passed. Looking to the sky, you see low, dark clouds and lightning flashes. You could call Evan and ask him to bring the sheep in, but you're not sure if the storm will hit you.

*To call Evan and have him bring the sheep in, turn to page 46.*

*To drive to the hilltop and observe the weather, turn to page 48.*

You pull your phone from your pocket. With a dirty fingertip, you tap the screen to call Evan. Mobile phones don't always work well out in the hills, but you are hopeful this morning.

The phone rings. Molly presses herself against your legs. She does that when she's nervous.

"Pick it up, you lazy cabbage," you mutter into the phone. You squat down to pat Molly's damp head.

The rain is coming down a little harder now, and you wish for your raincoat. It's hard not to envy your brother. You're getting wet and he's lying in bed, dry as a toasted bun.

After four rings, his voicemail message plays:

"How are ye? It's Evan. I'm busy and can't answer now. Message, please. Cheers."

*Busy? Hardly,* you think. *You're asleep!*

You hang up, unwilling to leave a message. You regret not waking him when you had the chance.

The clouds rumble, and Molly jumps up on the ATV seat. She looks ready to head back.

"It's just a wee bit of rain, Molly," you insist. "Down from there, now."

Moments later, you're not so sure. The wind is really picking up, and you see the trees in the valley sway.

The fence repairs shouldn't take long. You'd hate to lose any of your 42 sheep over a simple fix.

*Turn to page 50.*

You hadn't heard the weather was going to be rough today. The weather service usually does a fine job warning the island if severe weather is coming. You suspect nothing more than a small storm that will pass in an hour or so.

Even so, Molly is acting strange. She's done chasing critters and presses up against your leg.

You get on the ATV. "Up, my girl," you call to Molly, tapping your lap twice. She hurriedly hops up.

The dog presses against your chest. You find it odd that she's shivering. It's not cold, and her fur is thick.

"What's gotten into you?" you ask. Molly looks up, then gives you a quick lick on the chin. It's as though she doesn't want to talk about it.

You drive higher up into the hills. The ATV's big tires bounce over the stony ground. At the top of the biggest hill around, you stop the vehicle.

Molly glances at you as if she doesn't want to hop off here. "Down, Molly," you say, followed by a quick whistle. She obeys.

You climb up the hill and look out over the glens. The fields are lush and green beneath angry gray clouds. Lightning strikes farther out followed by a rumble of thunder.

The rain starts coming down a little harder now. Molly is back up on the ATV seat, ready to leave.

"We're not done here yet, girl," you say. "It's just a wee storm coming."

You're unsure you believe it yourself but know there's work to be done.

You climb back on the ATV and return to the broken fence.

*Turn to page 50.*

You spend a few minutes on the fence, wrapping wire around the new post in three spots. It's a quick fix, but it'll do. You still need to adjust the nearby posts to ensure nothing goes slack.

When you stand, you realize the rain has stopped. Even so, Molly whines. You know she's not hungry as she's eaten a proper breakfast.

The clouds are low and dark, but the color's a bit off, almost greenish. And it's calm, almost too calm.

There's a noise in the distance, like the engine from heavy machinery. You don't recognize it as any of your neighbor's farming equipment. Brennan's tractor is loud, but not like this.

"What is that?" you whisper to Molly and yourself.

Molly barks as if she's trying to tell you something.

In the distance thunder rumbles. Maybe it's moved on to somewhere else? You look at the fence. Nearly done.

The heavy engine sound grows louder. You think about your sheep out to pasture. If it's startling you, it's probably scaring them too. Molly looks anxious. Maybe you should go back to the farmhouse and return when the weather clears up.

*To stay in the field and finish fixing the fence, turn to page 52.*

*To head back to the farmhouse, turn to page 54.*

If you called it quits anytime a small, unexpected issue popped up, nothing would get done. You move to the next fence post and Molly follows, her tail between her legs.

You tighten the wire at the top of the post and adjust the second line. Dirt and sticks slap against the back of your work coat. Turning, you see an enormous funnel cloud out in the distance. A tornado is forming!

You would complain about the lack of warning sirens, but their noise doesn't reach this far out into the country. To be fair, you've had plenty of warning.

Molly barks as if saying *I told you so!*

The wind picks up. Branches crack above you. Leaves rush into the sky, forcing you to shield your face with your arm.

It's time to move, but you have a hard time going anywhere. The sight is incredible. Trees are ripped from the ground and torn apart like broccoli sprigs.

During a tornado, you know it's best to stay low. But it might be hard to find a low place up in the hills. You look at the ATV and wonder if you can make it back home.

*To find a low place, turn to page 60.*

*To ride back to the farmhouse, turn to page 62.*

You're unsure about the strange weather and the even stranger noise, but you don't like it. It's better to get home and safe inside than be out on the land. You jump on the ATV, turn the key, and start it up.

The wind grows stronger. You back up to steer the ATV toward home. Glancing to your left, you see a funnel cloud forming in the distance.

*A tornado!* your mind screams.

Molly jumps up onto your lap. She barks as if saying *Let's go, already!*

You race down the trail, feeling the wind whipping at you. Leaves and sticks are flying through the air hitting the ATV. Trees along the path whistle and sway. You're unsure which way the tornado will go, but hope it isn't headed your way. You go even faster.

When you reach the farmhouse, you see your brother in the doorway. He's clutching the doorframe like he might blow over.

Evan points toward the sky. "Storm's coming!" he shouts.

"Storm? It's a tornado!" you yell as you and Molly hop off and race to the door.

"The herd is in, right?" Evan shouts, pointing to the barn. It's hard to hear over the wind.

You look at their pen. It's empty, except for one. Your most stubborn sheep, Alice, searches for food scraps.

The two of you should try bringing the sheep back, but is there time?

*To herd the sheep back to their pen, turn to page 56.*

*To leave the sheep to survive on their own, turn to page 64.*

"We need to get them," you shout.

The two of you scramble, but Molly knows what's next. She dashes out into the field and disappears over the hill. The two of you follow.

The wind picks up and you and Evan shield your eyes from flying debris. A wooden post bounces along the ground.

*Another fence to fix,* you think.

At the top of the hill, you see Molly, and the sheep aren't far off. They stampede toward you, spooked by the weather.

"Walk up, Molly," you shout, giving her the command to bring the sheep your way.

Evan shrieks and you see him pointing. The tornado is bigger.

"It's getting closer!" he screams.

A large oak bends and crashes across the road.

You, Evan, Molly and the sheep race back toward the farmhouse. Alice looks up as you approach.

As you get closer, Molly runs back out toward the pasture.

"What is she doing?" Evan shouts.

You do a quick head count. There's a sheep missing. Molly went back out after the stray. The wind increases. The tornado is closer than ever.

*To bring the sheep to the barn, turn to page 58.*

*To go after Molly and bring her to safety, turn to page 66.*

You hate to leave Molly out there but know to trust your dog's instincts. You hope she and the lost sheep will be okay.

"Open the gate," you shout. Your voice feels lost in the storm. A small pebble strikes your cheek like a punch in the face.

“C’mon, then,” Evan cries. “We’re out of time!”

Your brother unlatches and opens the gate. The sheep are confused, startled by the storm. Without Molly to keep them in line, they’re wandering as if they’ve never done this before.

“Let’s go,” you shout. You nudge a few strays toward the larger group. “Keep together, will ya?” You lead the sheep toward the barn.

As you get closer, you hear the barn creaking. You’re unsure the barn will stay intact. To your right, the front door of the farmhouse bangs open against the wall. Maybe there’s a chance you could herd them in the front door.

*To continue and put the sheep in the barn, turn to page 68.*

*To bring the sheep into the farmhouse instead, turn to page 70.*

You don't know which way the tornado might head. You definitely doubt you'd get back to the farmhouse in time.

"Let's go, Molly," you say. She hops on the seat of the ATV, only to sense you're headed somewhere else.

You scan the area frantically, looking for shelter. Low places are in short supply. You and Molly scramble down a hill, crossing into your neighbor Brennan's property.

The wind really picks up, and you're running out of time. Molly darts off to the left and you follow. She's stopped at a nearly dry creek. It's not incredibly low, but it could work.

"Down, Molly!" you shout, getting down on your belly. Cold water soaks your shirt front and pants.

Molly lies down, and you put an arm around your beloved pet. With your free arm, you cover your head. The wind whips at the back of your clothes. They're flapping like a flag on a pole. Small bits of dirt and stones bounce off your body.

You lie flat for what feels like forever. Finally, the winds ease up. The storm is over.

You and Molly get up. You're both happy to be alive.

## THE END

To follow another path, turn to page 8.
To learn more about tornadoes,
turn to page 101.

You can't stay here. Not with a tornado coming. You've got a farm, a herd of sheep, and a brother to think about.

You leave your tools, hop on the ATV, and start it up, but the engine doesn't turn. You think of all of the movies where this kind of thing happens.

“Come on!” you shout. In your panic, you didn’t turn the key. You twist it, then press the start button. The ATV roars to life. You pat your leg for Molly to join you, but she’s already racing for home.

You speed along the trail. The wind strengthens, and you see the tornado has gotten closer. It’s a monster of a funnel, tearing its way through the fields. You struggle to keep control of the ATV.

The farmhouse seems farther away than usual. You’re unsure you’ll make it. Just then, you are blown off of your seat. You’re airborne and flying higher and higher.

As you fall back to earth, you see the small stone wall you and your brother built years ago. It’s the last thing you see.

## THE END

To follow another path, turn to page 8.
To learn more about tornadoes,
turn to page 101.

“We’ll never get them back here in time,” you shout. You move past your brother and into the farmhouse. Molly follows you, happy to be home and safe.

“You sure?” Evan asks. “Poor things . . .”

He stays in the doorway, scanning the horizon. The sky looks dark and foreboding as leaves and grit shoot through the front door.

“Close it up!” you shout. “We need to brace ourselves!”

The farmhouse is sturdy and made of stone, but you know it’s not indestructible. You remember to find a room without windows when a tornado strikes.

Evan closes the door. You can see he’s upset and scared.

“Over here,” you shout. The three of you crouch down in the hallway. The bathroom window at the end shows you the chaos outside.

Debris is flying everywhere. Heavy objects bang against the farmhouse. The frames on the walls above you rattle. A window breaks. Wind whips things around the kitchen.

And then, it's over.

You're unsure about the rest of the farm, but you, Evan, and Molly survived. You're not sure if the sheep did too. At least, not yet.

## THE END

To follow another path, turn to page 8.
To learn more about tornadoes,
turn to page 101.

“Get the sheep to shelter. I’m going after Molly,” you shout as you run off.

Your brother yells after you, but the wind mutes his voice. The wind makes it a struggle to climb the hill. More debris flies around. You squint to keep your eyes clear of dirt.

“Molly!” you shout, then whistle. The noise is lost in the wind. On the hilltop, you don’t see your dog or lost sheep anywhere.

The funnel cloud grows larger. Objects twist in its deadly winds. In no time, it will hit your farmhouse and the nearby house of your neighbor Brennan.

There’s a crash, and you see the barn has collapsed. A bark to your left reveals Molly and the sheep. They’re crouched low against a large rock in the field.

You run toward the two animals as leaves and loose dirt bounce off of you. You’re lifted off of your feet and tossed across the field like a ragdoll.

Every bone in your body feels broken as you lie on the ground, waiting for the storm to pass. Your eyes close, and you wonder if it's the end.

Moments later, something wet lashes across your cheek. You open your eyes to find Molly and the sheep standing over you.

You're injured, but alive. You hope no one else was hurt.

## THE END

To follow another path, turn to page 8.
To learn more about tornadoes,
turn to page 101.

There's no time to change plans. The barn will have to do for the sheep. Evan is at the large door, waving them into their pens. They don't seem as certain of the decision as you are. Bits of straw fly from the thatched roof.

"In ya go," Evan shouts. "Out of the storm."

You stay at the rear of the flock, keeping them in line. Their baas of protest fade into the howling wind and the noise of thousands of leaves rustling above. With the herd finally in place, Evan bolts the door.

"Let's batten down our own hatches," he says. You both race into the house.

Fighting the wind, you force the door closed. Evan helps you latch it tight. Small pebbles and bits of grass tap at the windows.

You're tempted to observe the barn from inside. But you also know to stay away from glass during a tornado. The best place to shelter is in a windowless room.

"The hallway," you suggest. You and Evan sit down, your backs against the wall.

There's a loud crash, followed by heavy objects hitting the house. You close your eyes, hoping your animals are safe.

When the storm passes, you get up and look outside.

The barn is destroyed, and all of your sheep are gone. There's a scratch at the door. Evan opens it, and Molly and the lost sheep come inside.

Four of you survived. You spend the rest of the day looking for the other sheep. Some are never found.

## THE END

To follow another path, turn to page 8.
To learn more about tornadoes,
turn to page 101.

You don't like how this all looks.

"That barn isn't standing long," you shout.

"What?" Evan cries. "So where—"

His voice fades as he follows your gaze to the farmhouse.

"Are you mad?" he asks.

Your brother likes to argue, but now isn't the time. Without delay, you nudge the sheep over to the house. They look unsure about heading somewhere they've never been.

"Help me!" you shout.

Evan does his part. With gentle prodding and shouting, the sheep file in through the front door, one at a time. You look around to make sure there aren't any strays.

You hear a bark. *Molly!* The dog and the lost sheep dash your way.

“To me, Molly,” you shout. She’s confused as sheep don’t go in the house. The heavy wind seems to remind her that rules don’t apply today.

Finally, the last sheep and Molly are in the house. You and Evan join them and force the door closed.

You guide the sheep away from the windows and funnel as many of them as you can into the hallway. It’s crowded and loud.

You and Evan crouch down low and hope for the best.

*Turn the page.*

In seconds, there's a loud crash. Heavy timbers strike the house. One shatters a kitchen window. Wind and glass fly around inside.

You, Evan, and your animals wait out the storm. When it passes, you get up.

The house is a mess, but everyone is safe. The barn, however, is completely destroyed.

Alice bleats. *Baaaa.*

You smile. The barn can be rebuilt. You're so grateful you, your brother, and the animals are safe. "Okay," you shout. "Everyone out!"

## THE END

To follow another path, turn to page 8.
To learn more about tornadoes,
turn to page 101.

CHAPTER 4

# A DRIVE IN THE COUNTRYSIDE

"Come on, it'll be fun!" your cousin Micaela insists. "It's just a few hours!"

Despite her promise, you don't really want to go. You've traveled 17 hours to get to her house in Posados, Argentina, to see her and your other cousin, Santino. Now she wants to take a three-hour road trip?

"We have waterfalls in the United States," you say. "Ever hear of Niagara Falls?"

"Psssh," Micaela scoffs. "Iguazu Falls makes Niagara Falls look like a leaky faucet!"

You look at Santino for support. Your cousin is the one with the car, after all.

*Turn the page.*

Iguazu Falls

He shrugs and smiles. "Iguazu is very impressive," he admits.

"But it's such a long drive," you whine.

"We can catch up," Micaela says. "And you'll get to see the countryside. You won't regret it."

"Okay," you say, giving in. "But it better be amazing."

It's decided. You hop in the back seat and Micaela sits up front with her brother. You're on your way.

The first hour of the trip is spent talking about college life. In the middle of a story about your chemistry class, rain comes down hard.

"Whoa," Santino cries. "Who knew there was a storm coming?"

He turns on his wipers. They whip back and forth.

"Adventure!" Micaela exclaims, smiling. You can tell she's afraid you and Santino will call the whole trip off.

"Ay, this rain," Santino cries. He's leaning forward as if to see better.

There are heavier taps on the roof of the car. Out the window you see small white pellets. They're little chunks of ice.

"Hail," you say.

The storm is pretty bad, but maybe it'll clear up. You're about an hour away from your cousins' house and two hours from Iguazu Falls. Either way, there is no quick escape.

*To ask Santino to turn around, turn to page 78.*

*To keep quiet, hoping it'll clear up, turn to page 80.*

"We should turn around," you suggest. Ultimately, it's not your decision, but you're not liking this storm.

Santino groans, then looks at Micaela.

"My paint job," he grumbles.

"How was I supposed to know it would hail?" Micaela snaps.

Santino turns the car around on the slick highway to head back to Elgabo.

You drive for a while, and just as suddenly as it started, the storm is over.

"Okay, that's strange," Santino says, scanning the sky. "It's totally calm now."

You peer up at the sky through the rain-dotted back window. There's a strange, almost greenish tint to it. The clouds are low and dark. There's a rumble in the distance. Thunder? You roll down your window.

You hear what sounds like a train chugging along the tracks. You scan both sides of the road. There aren't any train tracks that you can see. You realize what that means.

"Hey!" you shout, rolling up the window. "I think a tornado is coming!"

Micaela had turned the radio off to talk and catch up. When she turns it back on, your suspicions are confirmed. A prerecorded alert states a tornado has touched down just north of you.

"How far away is it? Do we keep driving?" Santino asks.

You're unsure where the tornado is. You've heard staying in a vehicle during a tornado is dangerous. But you're in the middle of the countryside. Where are you supposed to go?

*To ask Santino to keep driving, turn to page 90.*

*To tell everyone to leave the car and find shelter, turn to page 92.*

"It's just a storm," you say. "I'm sure it'll pass."

"Right," Micaela adds.

Santino sighs.

About ten more minutes into the trip, the hail and rain stop.

"That's it?" Santino says, surprised.

It seems oddly calm outside. Dark, low clouds loom above, but they seem okay. You can't see any funnel clouds so far. What you don't care for is the sky's greenish tint.

*Something isn't right*, you think, but you keep quiet.

As Micaela is telling you her fiftieth story, you stop her.

"Do you hear that?" you ask.

Micaela stops talking and listens. There's a machinery sound, like a train. You roll down the window. The sound seems louder and closer.

"What is that?" Santino asks.

"I think there's a tornado coming," you whisper.

You look around. There's a little cabin along the road. It might work for shelter. You're not sure where the tornado is. Maybe it's best to keep driving?

*To keep driving and hope the tornado is somewhere else, turn to page 82.*

*To get out and take shelter in the cabin, turn to page 94.*

"I say we keep driving," you suggest, rolling up the window. "That cabin looks too risky."

Santino nods and continues down the highway. The wind continues tossing things at the car. At one point, three metal garbage cans bounce across the road.

"See anything yet?" you ask. In the back seat, you can't see as much as your cousins.

"Nothing yet," Micaela says. She leans as far forward as her seat belt will allow.

You scan the flat countryside to your left. You see two small funnel clouds on the low-hanging clouds. *Are those tornadoes waiting to happen?* you wonder.

All three of you search for any sign of the tornado. You wonder if seeing one means it's too late.

Then it's quieter outside. Micaela opens her window. The loud engine noise is gone.

“It must be over,” she says. “I’m glad we didn’t turn around!”

Still, it’s calm outside. Too calm.

You know it can be super calm before a tornado strikes. Should you take cover? Or would it be better to drive to the next town?

*To ask Santino to stop the car so you all can take cover, turn to page 84.*

*To keep driving to the next town, turn to page 86.*

You know a tornado can form at any time. And you're worried about the funnel clouds you saw. If the sound you heard was a tornado, another could still come.

"Let's pull over," you say. "I've got a bad feeling."

"But there's no tornado," Micaela whines.

Santino pulls to the side of the road.

"This is dumb," Micaela protests, but she climbs out too.

The three of you are out of the car for two seconds before hearing the familiar train sound again.

"Another one is coming!" you shout over the noisy winds.

You run away from the car and your cousins follow. Pieces of bark, branches, and leaves kick up. You run through the grass, getting the legs of your pants wet.

You hurriedly look through a gap in the trees to the left. Off in the distance, you see a funnel cloud extend to the ground.

"Tornado!" Santino shouts, beating you to it.

You spot and point at a small trench up ahead. Your cousins nod. It's wet but you all get down as low as possible and cover your heads.

Debris flies over the top of you. A small rock crashes into your hand.

And then . . . it's quiet.

Is it over? It seems to be. You, Santino, and Micaela poke your heads out of the trench. You all look at each other in relief. After taking a few minutes to calm your nerves, the three of you get back in the car and drive.

*Turn to page 88.*

"We should keep going," you say. It might just seem calm because the wind has died down.

As you continue down the highway, you continue to watch the clouds. They look like they're turning and swirling. Or is it just your imagination? You're tired from traveling and nervous from the storm.

After a few more miles, Santino points to the side of the road.

"Look," he says.

You turn your head and see fallen trees lying on their sides with their roots exposed.

"Something big went through here," he says.

You see an overturned car along the side of the road. The roof is partially crushed. Thankfully, you don't see anyone inside. You hope they found a safe place to take shelter.

A large building for farming equipment has big chunks of twisted metal on its roof. A few men stand outside, looking at the damage.

"This is bad," you think, seeing more destruction the farther you drive. You're glad you didn't leave Elgabo earlier. You might've been caught in the tornado's path.

*Turn to page 88.*

As you and your cousins continue along the highway, something occurs to you.

"Are there tornado sirens in Argentina?" you ask.

"No," Micaela says. "I don't think so."

"That's right," Santino confirms. "I've never heard them."

In another 20 minutes, you spot a town ahead. People are running across the street. Wind suddenly roars at the side of the car. Loose objects are flying everywhere.

"Oh no, no, no," you whisper. You're finding it hard to catch your breath.

To your left, another tornado has formed. You see it carving its way toward the town.

In mere moments, you feel the tires sliding sideways on the road.

"We need to get out of the car," Santino shouts.

"There's a supermercado," Micaela cries. She points to a grocery store just off the road. You see people inside watching the approaching storm from behind a large window. A little closer to you, metal dumpsters are chained to a post. You need to move. Now.

*To hide in a dumpster to protect yourself from flying debris, turn to page 96.*

*To run into the supermarket, turn to page 98.*

"Let's keep driving," you suggest to Santino. "I'd hate to be out in the open if a tornado's coming."

You look out the back window. The sky is still an odd shade of green. The trees along the side of the road sway back and forth. Leaves and sticks tumble across the highway.

"This is terrible," Micaela insists, turning the radio off. "I really wanted you to see the falls."

"Yeah, me too," you reply and feel bad. *But I'd much rather live to try again someday,* you think.

The sky ahead is clear but you're not sure for how long. It's quite possible the tornado might move toward Elgabo. You've heard tornadoes can change direction and last anywhere from a few seconds to an hour.

Knowing your cousins' house is less than an hour away makes you feel better. Just a bit, anyway.

You make it back to Micaela and Santino's house. While it's nice to visit with your cousins, nothing else nearly as exciting as a tornado happens during your stay. And you're okay with that!

## THE END

To follow another path, turn to page 8.
To learn more about tornadoes,
turn to page 101.

"We should get out of the car," you say. "Let's find shelter and wait it out."

"We haven't even seen the tornado," Micaela says, looking at you funny.

"The radio said one touched down," Santino replies. He's scanning the windshield to see if he can spot it.

"They move pretty quickly," you add. "If we wait until we see it, it might be too late."

Santino pulls over and the three of you pause a moment. The wind is picking up, launching loose debris at the car from all angles.

You look out the window and point to a spot near an old, abandoned building. It looks like it was once a motel. There's a chain-link fence surrounding something.

"Follow me," you say. "Let's go!"

All three of you pop out of the car and dash to the fenced area. The wind grows stronger by the second. As you get closer, you see it's a mostly empty swimming pool. There's greenish sludge and trash at the bottom.

*It'll have to do,* you think.

"I'm not going in there," Santino says.

"I don't like it either," you say, jumping in. Micaela follows.

"Tino!" she shouts. "Get in!"

Santino gets in. You move against the wall to a ladder in the deep end. It's bolted into the side of the pool. You hang onto it for dear life.

The tornado comes close but misses you. You're filthy and wet but happy to be alive.

## THE END

To follow another path, turn to page 8.
To learn more about tornadoes,
turn to page 101.

You don't like being in the car, since you know tornadoes can change directions quickly. You tap Santino's shoulder from the back seat and point.

"Let's find some shelter," you say. "That place might work!"

Santino pulls over and the three of you get out. You run through the whipping winds, shielding your faces.

You reach the old cabin. The front door hangs open on rusty hinges.

"Let's get in the basement," you shout over the howling wind.

"Basement?" Micaela says. "I don't think . . ."

Your heart sinks. There probably isn't a basement here. Basements aren't as common as they are in the midwestern United States.

You hear a loud snap and a crash. A nearby tree splits in two.

“The tornado’s close!” Santino shouts. He pushes you and Micaela inside. He tries to pull the warped door shut behind him.

The entire cabin shakes and creaks. You look for something to hold onto. There’s nothing inside the small space.

A second later, the entire cabin is demolished. You and your cousins are thrown hundreds of feet. Heavy wood from the cabin hits you in the head hard. You’re dead before you hit the ground.

## THE END

To follow another path, turn to page 8.
To learn more about tornadoes,
turn to page 101.

“Run for the dumpsters,” you shout. You launch the door open and run, your cousins close behind. A moment later, Santino’s car flips over, barely missing the three of you. It tumbles toward the supermarket in a mess of twisted steel and broken glass.

A moment later, the front window of the supermarket shatters. You hear screaming.

The wind pushes you forward. You tumble and fall to the ground. Micaela helps you up. Finally, the three of you reach the dumpsters. Santino holds open the lid of one and you climb in, helping your cousins in too.

Santino closes the lid and the three of you crouch. The stink is enough to make your eyes water.

You feel and hear heavy objects slam against the metal sides. The whole dumpster shifts, but then stops, caught by the chain.

Something crashes above and part of the dumpster's lid caves in. You close your eyes and hope that all of you stay safe.

After a few minutes, it's quiet again. The rain has stopped. Something squeaks above you. The bent lid opens, and daylight streams into the dumpster. Someone reaches in to help you.

The storm is over, and the three of you survived. You may not have seen the falls, but you lived to make the trek another day.

## THE END

To follow another path, turn to page 8.

To learn more about tornadoes, turn to page 101.

The supermarket seems like the best bet.

"The market!" you shout. "Go!"

You shove the car door open and run as fast as you can toward the market. Chunks of destroyed trees, signs, and crates fly through the air. As you get closer to the market, you hear a metallic crunch.

"My car!" Santino shouts and turns to see.

You only realize he's stopped once you reach the open door. As you urge him to run, the wind picks him up. You and Micaela are thrown into the supermarket's entrance. Santino is thrown too, but not through the door.

He smashes through the big window and slams against a shelf.

You and Micaela get up, stunned from your tumble. You head over to check on Santino and see the looks of horror on the survivors' faces.

Santino didn't make it.

## THE END

To follow another path, turn to page 8.
To learn more about tornadoes,
turn to page 101.

CHAPTER 5

# TWISTING TORNADOES

Tornadoes are among the most deadly and powerful natural forces on Earth. All tornadoes start with a thunderstorm, but not all thunderstorms create tornadoes. When the winds from a thunderstorm vary greatly in direction and speed, an updraft will build and begin to rotate. The rotating updraft pulls in more warm air from the thunderstorm, increasing its rotation speed. Soon, a funnel cloud begins to form. The funnel builds up strength, stretches, and becomes longer. As the funnel cloud pulls up debris and dirt, its true shape appears. When the twisting funnel cloud touches the ground, it's officially a tornado.

Tornadoes are measured on the Enhanced Fujita Scale, or EF Scale, named after Dr. Tetsuya Theodore Fujita. The scale was originally developed in 1971 and updated in 2007 to measure the amount of destruction a tornado leaves behind. An EF0 is on the weak end of the scale with winds ranging from 65–85 miles (105–137 kilometers) per hour. An EF5 is the strongest with winds reaching more than 200 miles (322 km) per hour.

Dr. Tetsuya Fujita with a tornado simulator

## EF SCALE

| Rating | Wind Speed (mph) | Damage |
|---|---|---|
| EF0 | 65-85 | minor roof, branches |
| EF1 | 86-110 | broken windows |
| EF2 | 111-135 | roofs off, large trees |
| EF3 | 136-165 | homes damaged |
| EF4 | 166-200 | homes leveled |
| EF5 | 200+ | incredible damage |

TORNADO RATING

Tornadoes can occur anywhere on the planet, but most of them happen in the central area of the United States. For this reason, this region was nicknamed Tornado Alley. There is no official boundary for Tornado Alley. Parts of Texas, Oklahoma, Kansas, and Nebraska are usually included. It may also include sections of Missouri, South Dakota, Iowa, and other states. The United States gets about 1,000 tornadoes every year. That's 75 percent of the world's known tornadoes!

No two tornadoes are the same. They can come in many different shapes and sizes. The speed in which they travel varies too. Some are slow and don't appear to be moving at all. Others can travel as fast as 60 miles (97 km) per hour. Don't judge a tornado's destructive power by its size and speed, though. Even small and slow tornadoes can cause a lot of damage.

Despite their force, most tornadoes only last about ten minutes. However, some can last for over an hour. A tornado usually breaks apart when it travels over colder areas or when the clouds above it separate.

Meteorologists help warn people ahead of time if tornado conditions are forming. They use radar, satellites, and weather balloons to watch weather patterns. The data they collect helps meteorologists forecast dangerous weather conditions.

Tornadoes may be an awesome event of nature, but they're incredibly dangerous. Paying attention to severe weather warnings and sirens can keep you safe from these swirling storms.

# TRUE TORNADO SURVIVAL STORIES

In 2024, Jeff Frederickson and his wife were transporting their family's 1971 Ford Thunderbird car from Minnesota to Texas. While passing through Marietta, Oklahoma, a massive tornado hit. Jeff told his wife to run to the ditch on her side of the road, and he'd get to the ditch on the other side. A semitruck next to him was bouncing up and down as the tornado got close. Debris struck him as he headed for the ditch. Jeff suffered 13 broken ribs, a big head wound, and a split thumb. His wife survived with minor injuries.

In 2013, Gavin Hodgson of New South Wales, Australia, was driving his truck around his farm. A tornado with winds reaching 155 miles (249 km) per hour hit his house and shed right in front of him. With no time to lose, he crouched down in his truck. He tucked his head under the glove box and held onto the gear shifter. The tornado picked up his truck with Gavin inside. The next thing he knew, the truck slammed against a utility pole and slid down to the ground. Luckily, Gavin survived the tornado.

In 1999, a massive EF5 tornado struck the Bridge-Creek Moore area of Oklahoma. It destroyed the home of Amy Crago, who was holding her 11-month-old daughter, Aleah. The winds picked up and tossed Amy around, forcing her to drop her baby. In a matter of moments, Aleah was gone. As the mother was rushed to the hospital, she begged a deputy to find her baby. People feared Aleah was dead. Hours later, a nurse asked Amy if she was the one missing the baby. Aleah had been found alive, lying face down in mud about 100 feet (30 meters) from her home. Because she was covered in mud, Aleah was given the nickname "Mud Baby."

# TORNADO SURVIVAL KIT

A tornado can strike when you least expect it. Having a tornado kit ready will save you time and maybe even your life.

**backpack**–to hold supplies

**bottled water**–at least 1 gallon (3.8 liters) per person

**non-perishable food** Don't forget a can opener!

**flashlight and batteries**

**first aid kit containing**

- bandages
- first aid creams
- alcohol wipes/disinfectant wipes

**toilet paper**

Bring bags that can be sealed for bathroom waste.

**sleeping bag/blankets**

**multi-tool**

**wrench and pliers**

**whistle**–to signal for help and rescue

# STAYING SAFE IN A TORNADO

### Know where to go

Plan where to go in case of a tornado emergency ahead of time. A basement or tornado shelter is best. If neither of those are available, get inside the lowest level of a building and stay away from windows.

### Protect yourself

Sit or crouch down low and cover your head. Use blankets and furniture to act as a shield around you.

### If stuck in a car

It's best to get out of a car. But if that's not possible, keep your seat belt on and bend down so your head is below the windows. Cover and protect your head.

### If outside with no shelter nearby

Lie down flat in a low-level area such as a ditch and cover your head with your arms and hands.

### Do not:

- Seek shelter under bridges.
- Try to outrun a tornado.
- Run outside to see the tornado.
- Look out or open windows.

# GLOSSARY

**debris** (duh-BREE)—scattered pieces left after something has been destroyed

**locomotive** (low-kuh-MOW-tuhv)—a self-propelled vehicle that runs on rails and pulls railroad cars

**meteorologist** (mee-tee-ur-OL-oh-jist)—a scientist who studies the Earth's atmosphere to predict and understand the planet's weather

**PA system** (pee-AY SISS-tuhm)—abbreviation for public address system; a PA system includes a loudspeaker so people in the surrounding area can hear you

**partition** (par-TI-shuhn)—a structure that separates or divides a space into parts

**pavilion** (puh-VIL-yun)—an open structure in a park used for entertainment or shelter

**updraft** (UHP-draft)—a strong upward air current

# READ MORE

Brink, Tracy Vonder. *Tornadoes.* New York: Crabtree Publishing, 2023.

Manning, Matthew K. *Can You Survive the 1925 Tri-State Tornado?: An Interactive History Adventure*. North Mankato, MN: Capstone, 2023.

Mason, Jenny. *Surviving a Tornado.* Minnetonka, MN: Kaleidoscope Books, 2021.

# INTERNET SITES

*Ducksters: Weather: Tornadoes*
ducksters.com/science/earth_science/tornadoes.php

*Kiddle: Tornado Facts for Kids*
kids.kiddle.co/Tornado

*National Geographic Kids: Tornadoes*
kids.nationalgeographic.com/science/article/tornado

# ABOUT THE AUTHOR

Thomas Kingsley Troupe is the author of over 200 books for young readers. He's written books about everything from werewolves, talking spaceships, and ballerinas to even dirt. That's right, dirt. Thomas wrote his first book when he was in second grade and has been making up stories ever since. When he's not behind the keyboard, he enjoys reading, playing video games, and hunting ghosts with the Twin Cities Paranormal Society. Otherwise, he's probably taking a nap or something. Also, he loves cookies. TKT lives in Woodbury, MN, with his two sons.